Anonymous

Travellers' Guide

New York

Anonymous

Travellers' Guide
New York

ISBN/EAN: 9783337211455

Printed in Europe, USA, Canada, Australia, Japan

Cover: Foto ©Lupo / pixelio.de

More available books at **www.hansebooks.com**

TRAVELLERS' GUIDE NEW YORK

A.S. LEHMAIER, Manager.

1883

THE TRAVELLERS' GUIDE, containing in condensed form the prominent points of interest in the City of New York, as well as the addresses of the leading business establishments in the various branches of commerce, will, as the publisher believes, prove to strangers visiting the Metropolis a valuable aid in attending to their business in this city without the loss of time which, in the absence of such a publication as the present, has been unavoidable. In presenting this book to the public the publisher therefore trusts that he has supplied a long felt need.

CITY HALL SQUARE.

4

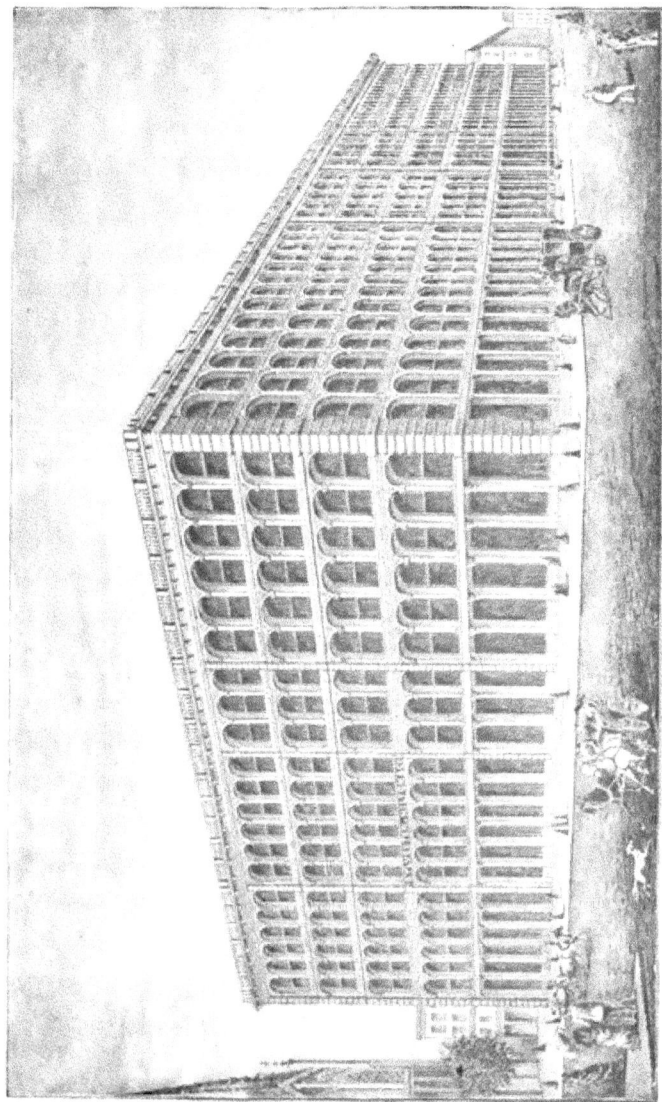

THE STEWART WAREHOUSE BUILDING   BROADWAY, 4TH AVENUE,
NINTH AND TENTH STREETS, N. Y.

SYLVESTER, HILTON, & CO., } Successors
E. J. DENNING, & CO., } Successors

NATIONAL BANK OF THE REPUBLIC,
BROADWAY AND WALL STREET.

Capital, - - - - - - - - $1,500,000
Surplus, - - - - - - - - $750,000

H. W. FORD, *President.*
T. T. BUCKLEY, *Vice-President.*
E. H. PULLEN, *Cashier.*

CHATHAM NATIONAL BANK OF NEW YORK,
196 BROADWAY

Capital, - - - - - - $450,000
Surplus and Profits, - - - - - $220.600

HENRY P. DOREMUS,   GEO. M. HARD,   FREDERICK WIEBUSCH,
Cashier.   *President.*   *Vice-President.*

CHEMICAL NATIONAL BANK,
270 BROADWAY.

Capital, - - - - - - - - $300,000
Surplus and Profit, - - - - $3,750,000

GEO. G. WILLIAMS, *President.*
W. J. QUINLAN, JR., *Cashier.*

EAST RIVER NATIONAL BANK,
682 BROADWAY.

Capital, - - - - - - - $250,000
Surplus, - - - - - - $90,100
CHARLES JENKINS, *President.*   ZENAS E. NEWELL, *Cashier.*

GARFIELD NATIONAL BANK OF NEW YORK,
COR. SIXTH AVE. AND 23D STREET.

Capital, - $200,000   Surplus, - - $25,000

GEO. H. ROBINSON, *Prest.*   A. C. CHENEY, *Vice-Prest.*   GEO. F. VAIL, *Cashier.*
DIRECTORS:

HENRY A. HURLBUT.   JOS. W. DREXEL.   EDWARD R. BELL.   HIRAM HITCHCOCK.   J. COLEMAN DRAYTON.
A. C. CHENEY.   THOS. D. ADAMS.   JOHN B. KITCHING.   JOHN J. McCOOK.   JOHN D. PRINCE.
G. H. ROBINSON.

6

LIVERPOOL & LONDON & GLOBE INSURANCE CO.
45, 47, 49, WILLIAM STREET.

GALLATIN NATIONAL BANK,

36 WALL STREET.

Capital,	$1,000,000
Surplus,	$905,000

FREDERICK D. TAPPEN, *President.*

ARTHUR W. SHERMAN, *Cashier.*

MERCHANTS' EXCHANGE NATIONAL BANK,

OF THE CITY OF NEW YORK,

257 BROADWAY.

Capital, $1,000,000

WM. A. THOMSON,	JOHN G. DAVIS,	ALLEN S. APGAR,
President.	*Vice-President.*	*Cashier.*

This Bank was chartered in the year 1829. Reorganized under the National Banking Laws in 1865. Over fifty years continued business.

Collections made at all accessible points throughout the United States. Accounts of Merchants, Banks and Bankers solicited.

NEW YORK NATIONAL EXCHANGE BANK,

136 CHAMBERS ST. (cor. College Place.)

Capital, $300,000. Surplus, $105,000

W. B. HALSTEAD,	DAVID D. ACKER,	C. B. OUTCALT,
President.	*Vice-President.*	*Cashier.*

SECOND NATIONAL BANK,

OF THE CITY OF NEW YORK,

FIFTH AVENUE, CORNER TWENTY-THIRD STREET.

Designated Depository of the United States.

CAPITAL, $300,000. SURPLUS, $135,000

JOHN C. ENO, *President.*   O. D. ROBERTS, *Cashier.*

THE MERCANTILE NATIONAL BANK,

OF THE CITY OF NEW YORK,

191 BROADWAY.

Capital,	$1,000,000
Surplus and Profits,	257,100

WM. P. ST. JOHN, *President*   FREDERICK B. SCHENCK, *Cashier.*

8

UNITED BANK BUILDING.

FIRST NATIONAL BANK, }
BANK OF THE REPUBLIC, } Wall Street and Broadway.

NATIONAL PARK BANK,

214 AND 216 BROADWAY.

Capital, - - - - - - - $2,000,000
Surplus, - - - - - 1,200,000

GEORGE H. POTTS,   E. K. WRIGHT,   C. I. DeBAUN,
President.   *Cashier.*   *Ass't Cashier.*

TRADESMEN'S NATIONAL BANK,

291 BROADWAY.

Capital, - - - - - $1,000,000
Surplus and Profits, - - - - - 308,000

RICHARD BERRY,   NATHANIEL NILES,   OLIVER F. BERRY,
President.   *Vice-President.*   *Cashier.*

United States National Bank,

33 NASSAU STREET.

Capital and Surplus, - - - - $650,000

H. V. NEWCOMB, *President.*   L. C. MURRAY, *Vice-President*
E. G. SHERMAN, *Cashier.*   H. M. HOYT, Jr., *Ass't Cashier.*

ST. NICHOLAS BANK,

7 WALL STREET.

Capital, - - - - - $500,000
Surplus and Profits, - - - 350,000

ARTHUR B. GRAVES, *President.*
THOS. C. POLLOCK, *Cashier.*

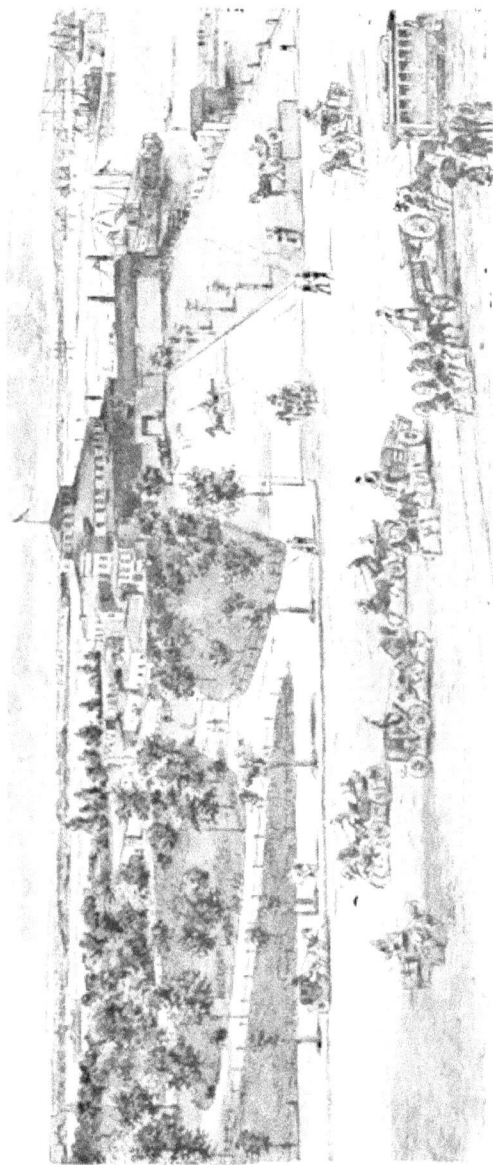

CASTLE GARDEN.

BANK OF THE METROPOLIS,

BROADWAY AND 15TH STREET.

Capital, - - $300,000.   Surplus and Profits, $101,000

ROBERT SCHELL, *Pres't.*   G. M. GROVES, *Vice-Pres't.*   THEO. ROGERS, *Cashier.*

NORTH RIVER BANK,

187 GREENWICH STREET,

Cor. Dey Street.

Capital, ... $240,000
Surplus, ... 75,000

LEVI APGAR, *President.*

E. E. GEDNEY, *Cashier.*

W. A. PULLMAN,   S. G. BAYNE,   S. G. NELSON,
  President.   *Vice-President.*   *Cashier.*

SEABOARD BANK,

Capital, $500,000.

18 BROADWAY, - - - NEW YORK.

We solicit Correspondence and the Accounts of Banks, Bankers, Merchants, Corporations, etc.

Three per cent. interest allowed to Banks whose accounts may warrant it.

CANADIAN BANK OF COMMERCE,

16 EXCHANGE PLACE.

Capital, - - $6,000,000.   Surplus, - $1,650,000

J. H. GOADBY AND B. E. WALKER, AGENTS.

MERCHANTS' BANK OF CANADA,

61 WALL STREET.

Capital, - - $5,700,000.   Reserve, $750,000

HENRY HAGUE AND JOHN B. HARRIS, JR., AGENTS.

12

MARINE NATIONAL BANK,
78 & 80 WALL STREET.

JAMES D. FISH, President.   JOHN D. FISH, Cashier.

14

CENTURY BUILDING,
33. 35. 37. E. 17TH ST.

THE MERCANTILE SAFE DEPOSIT CO.

EQUITABLE BUILDING, 118 to 124 Broadway, cor. Cedar St.

One of the Oldest Companies.

President,
LYMAN RHOADES.
Vice-Presidents,
GEO. D. MORGAN, HENRY B. HYDE.
Secretary,
ELMER M. BILLINGS.
Treasurer,
GEORGE BOSCAWEN.

Safes for Securities,
Storage for Valuables.

PRIVATE READING ROOMS,

OFFICE HOURS,
9 a. m. to 4:30 p. m.

Ladies' Department separate from the Main Offices.

HERRING'S SAFES

THE WORLD'S CHAMPIONS!

Medals Awarded at International Exhibitions.

1851	LONDON,
1853	PARIS,
1867	NEW YORK,
1876	PHILADELPHIA,
1878	SYDNEY, N.S.W.,
1879	MELBOURNE,
1880	ETC.

HERRING & CO. 251 & 252 Broadway. New York.

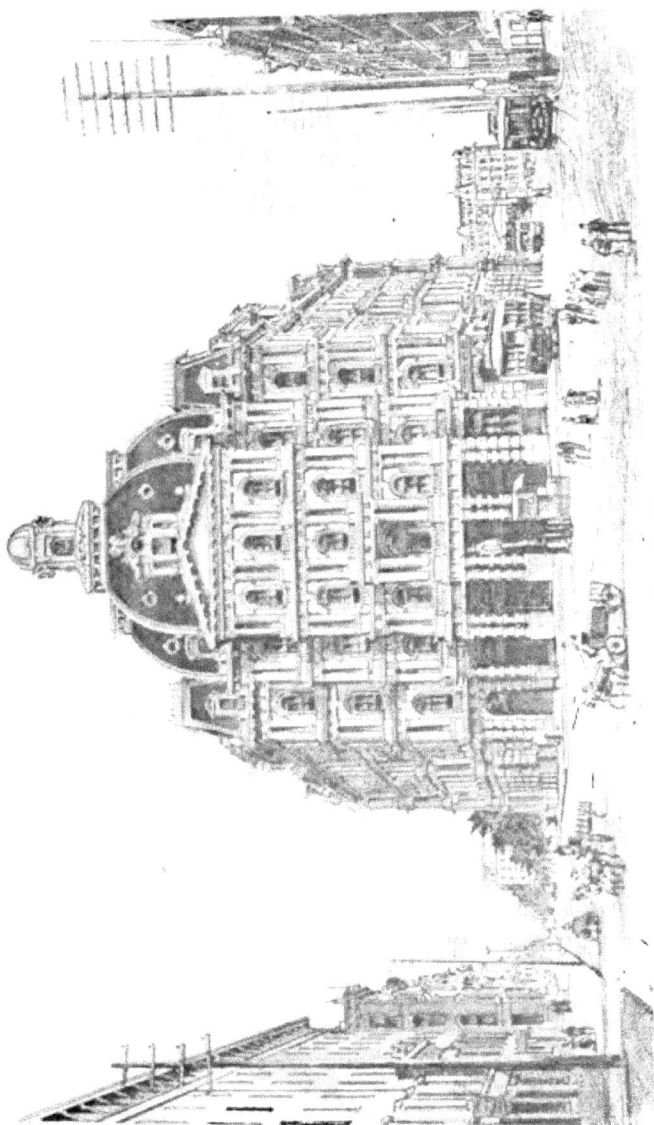

POST OFFICE.

THE GRAND UNION HOTEL,
SARATOGA SPRINGS, N. Y.

HENRY CLAIR, Lessee.

Cammann & Co.,

BANKERS,

No. 9 PINE STREET, · · · · NEW YORK.

HAROLD CLEMENS. A. P. FUNK.

Harold Clemens & Co.,
BANKERS,
"WELLES BUILDING," 18 & 20 BROADWAY.

Stocks, Bonds and Petroleum Bought and Sold on Commission.

Collins, Bouden & Jenkins,

BANKERS,

25 PINE STREET, · · · · · NEW YORK.

Decker, Howell & Co.,

BANKERS,

58 BROADWAY, COR. EXCHANGE PLACE, NEW YORK.

GRANT & WARD,
Bankers,
No. 2 WALL STREET, NEW YORK.

P. W. Gallaudet & Co.
BANKERS,
UNITED BANK BUILDING, WALL ST., COR. BROADWAY.

STOCKS, BONDS AND COMMERCIAL PAPER. Stocks and bonds bought and sold on commission at New York Stock Exchange. Advances made on business paper and other securities.

STANDARD OIL CO'S BUILDING,
46 BROADWAY.

Leopold Cahn & Co.,

BANKERS AND BROKERS,

No. 47 EXCHANGE PLACE, - - - NEW YORK.

LEOPOLD CAHN.   CHARLES NEUKIRCH.   J. S. BACHE.

M. E. De Rivas & Co.,

BANKERS AND BROKERS,

66 BROADWAY AND 19 NEW STREET, NEW YORK.

R. H. Parks & Co.,

BANKERS AND BROKERS,

Stocks, Grain, Cotton, etc.   13 NEW ST. & 72 B'WAY, NEW YORK.

We have an exclusively private Wire to Chicago.

Samuel A. Strang,

BANKER AND MERCHANT,

30 PINE STREET.

Vanderhoof, Morrison & Co.,

BANKERS AND STOCK COMMISSION BROKERS,

36 NEW STREET, NEW YORK.

S. V. White & Co.,

BANKERS AND BROKERS,

8 AND 10 WALL STREET, - - - NEW YORK.

HALSTED, HAINES & CO.,
IMPORTERS AND JOBBERS OF DRY GOODS,
376 & 378 BROADWAY (cor. of White Street), NEW YORK.

NEW YORK AND BROOKLYN BRIDGE.

Daniel A. Moran,

BANKER AND BROKER,

27 PINE STREET, . . NEW YORK.

FIRST-CLASS RAILROAD, STATE AND MUNICIPAL BONDS.

Chs. Minzesheimer & Co.,

BANKERS & BROKERS,

No. 8 WALL STREET, NEW YORK.

Connected by Private Wire with Branch Office, No. 335 Broadway.

Mitchell, Brouwer & Co.,

BROKERS,

No. 2 WALL ST., ROOM 20, - - - NEW YORK.

ELIHU C. MITCHELL, GEO. H. BROUWER, GEO. W. McGOWN.
Member of N. Y. Stock Exchange

Prince & Whitely,

STOCK BROKERS,

No. 64 BROADWAY, ... NEW YORK.

BRANCH OFFICE. 180 5TH AVE.

. Buy and sell on commission all classes of Railway and Mining Securities.

F. E. TROWBRIDGE,

BANKER AND BROKER,

Nos. 3 & 5 BROAD OR 27 WALL STREETS, ROOMS No. 25, 26 & 27,
DREXEL BUILDING, NEW YORK.

Miscellaneous Securities, Government, City, County, Town and Rail Road Bonds and Stocks
Bought and Sold on Commission or Carried on Margin. MEMBER OF THE N.Y. STOCK EXCHANGE.

CHAS. G. WOLFF. M. LEVY.

Chas. G. Wolff & Co.,

BANKERS AND BROKERS,

44 EXCHANGE PLACE, . NEW YORK.

VAN VLECK & CO.'S
CALIFORNIA AND OREGON LINES, CLIPPER SHIPS,
Pier 15, East River.   100 WALL STREET, NEW YORK.

MILLS OF BARBOUR
FLAX SPINNING CO.,
PATERSON, NEW JERSEY.

BARBOUR'S FLAX THREADS,
ALL KINDS FOR
HAND AND MACHINE WORK.
ALSO
Barbour's Macramé Lace Flax Threads.

THE BARBOUR BROTHERS CO.,

134 Church Street, New York.
25 High Street, Boston.
517 and 519 Market Street, San Francisco.

28

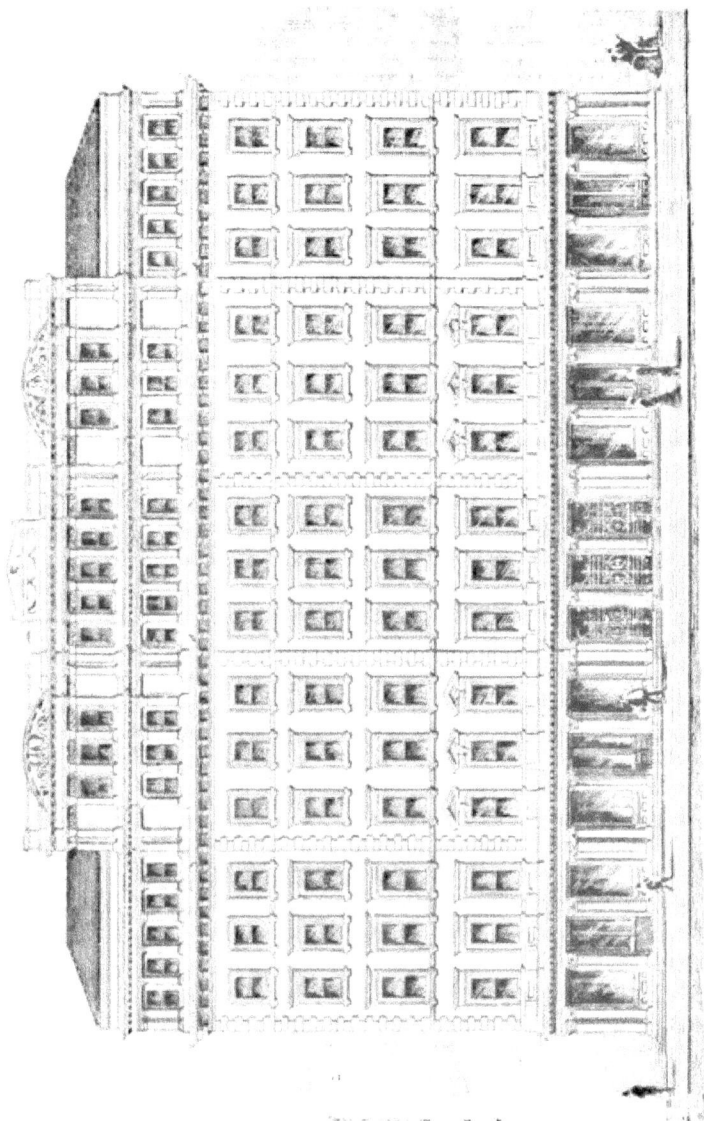

THE STEWART OFFICE BUILDING,

BROADWAY, CHAMBERS AND REAPE STREETS, NEW YORK.

Broadway Front.

30

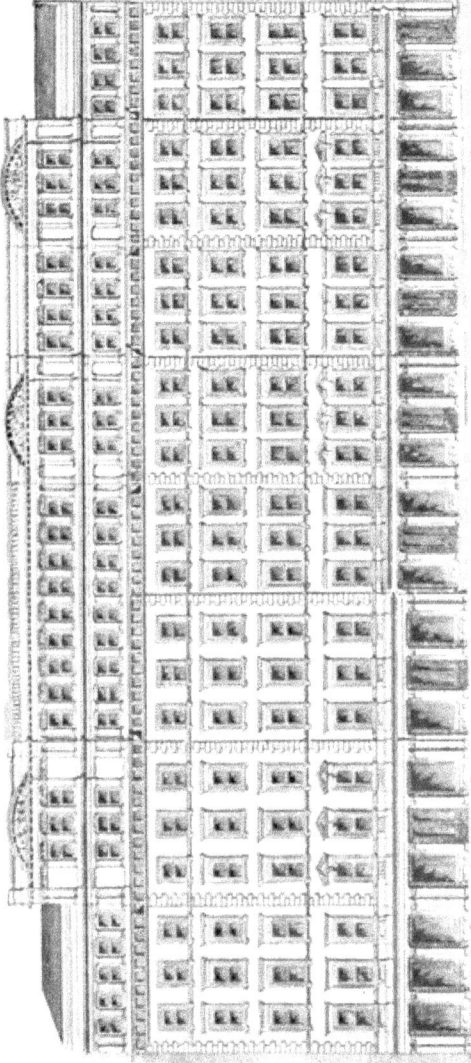

THE STEWART OFFICE BUILDING,

BROADWAY, CHAMBERS AND READE STREETS, NEW YORK.

Chambers Street Front.

BOLTING CLOTH.

DUFOUR & CO'S CELEBRATED

"Old Anchor Brand"

Is acknowledged by Millers to be superior in strength and regularity of mesh to all others.

For Sale by all first-class Mill Furnishers.

R. P. CHARLES,

13 South William Street.

Yard, Nos. 572 and 574 Washington Street.

O. A. GAGER,

SUCCESSOR TO CHAS. FIELD, HAVILAND & CO.

IMPORTER OF

French China & Fancy Pottery,

29 BARCLAY STREET,

NEW YORK.

Joseph J. O'Donohue.   Joseph J. O'Donohue, Jr.

JOSEPH J. O'DONOHUE & SON,

Importers and Dealers in

COFFEES AND TEAS,

101 Front Street, - New York.

THE CHINA AND JAPAN TRADING CO. (Limited)

34, 36 & 38 Burling Slip, New York.

Authorized Capital, $2,000,000.   Paid up Capital, $700,000.

W. H. Fogg, President.   J. F. Twombly, Vice-President.

George H. Burritt, Treasurer.

BRANCHES:

YOKOHAMA, KOBE-OSACA AND NAGASAKI, JAPAN ;

SHANGHAI, CHINA ; LONDON, ENGLAND.

Shipping and commission merchants ; importers and dealers in *Raw Silk, Teas* and *Productions generally* of China, Japan and the East, are prepared through their branches and Head office to execute orders and receive consignments of all descriptions of merchandise, which are respectfully solicited.

32

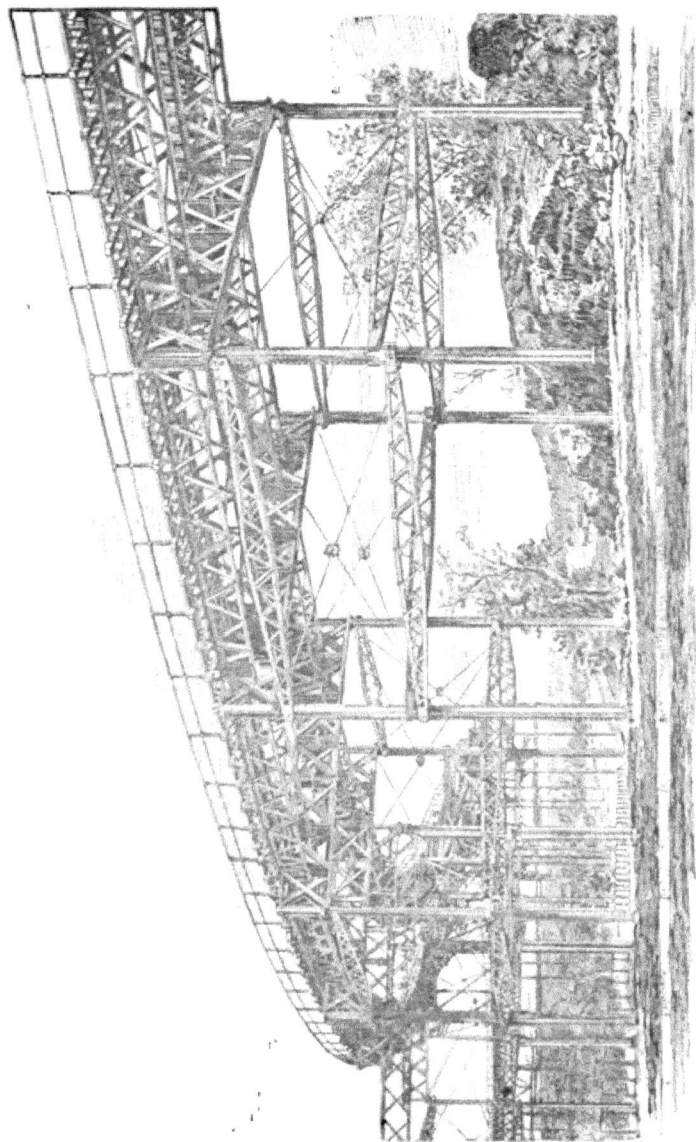

SECTION OF METROPOLITAN ELEVATED RAILROAD,
110TH STREET—EIGHTH AVENUE.

34

THE PARK AVENUE HOTEL.

PARK AVENUE, 32D AND 33D STREETS, NEW YORK.

MITCHELL, VANCE & CO.,
GAS FIXTURES, LAMPS, CLOCKS AND BRONZES,
836 AND 838 BROADWAY.

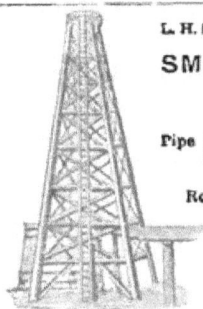

BATES, REED & COOLEY.
IMPORTERS AND JOBBERS OF DRY GOODS,
343, 345 & 347 BROADWAY (cor. of Leonard Street), NEW YORK.

Howard Fleming,

VIEW UP BROADWAY.

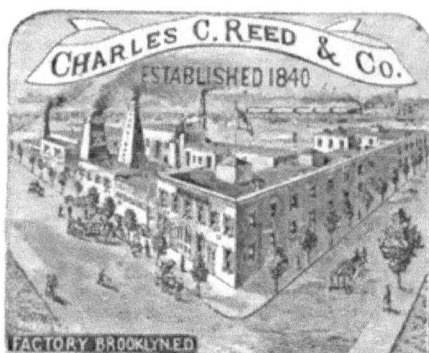

GALLATIN NATIONAL BANK,
36 WALL STREET.

Frederick D. Tappen, President.   Arthur W. Sherman, Cashier.

ATLANTIC
MUTUAL INSURANCE CO.,

NEW YORK.

OFFICE, 51 WALL STREET.

ORGANIZED 1842.

INSURES AGAINST MARINE AND INLAND NAVIGATION RISKS, AND WILL ISSUE POLICIES MAKING LOSS PAYABLE IN ENGLAND AND FRANCE.

ASSETS FOR THE SECURITY OF ITS POLICIES ARE MORE THAN

TEN MILLION DOLLARS.

The profits of the Company revert to the assured, and are divided annually, upon the premiums terminated during the year, certificates for which are issued, bearing interest in accordance with its charter.

J. D. JONES, President.   CHARLES DENNIS, Vice-President.
W. H. H. MOORE, 2d Vice-President.   A. A. RAVEN, 3d Vice-President.
J. H. CHAPMAN, Secretary.

United States Trust Company of New York,

NO. 49 WALL STREET.

Capital and Surplus,   -   -   - $5,000,000.00

This Company is a legal depository for moneys paid into Court, and is authorized to act as guardian or receiver of estates.

INTEREST ALLOWED ON DEPOSITS,

which may be made at any time and withdrawn after five days' notice, and will be entitled to interest for the whole time they may remain with the Company.

Executors, Administrators, or Trustees of Estates, and Females unaccustomed to the transaction of business, as well as Religious and Benevolent Institutions, will find this Company a convenient depository for money.

JOHN A. STEWART, *President.*   WILLIAM H. MACY, *Vice-President.*

Trustees :

INSURANCE BUILDINGS,
Atlantic Mutual Insurance Co.   United States Trust Co.
49 and 51 Wall Street, New York.

GEORGE H. CLARK & CO.,
Successors to CLARK BROTHERS,

HAT WAREHOUSE,
622 & 624 Broadway and 156 & 158 Crosby Street.

OBELISK,
CENTRAL PARK.

TEFFT, WELLER & CO.,
IMPORTERS AND JOBBERS OF DRY GOODS,
324 — 330 BROADWAY, NEW YORK.

SEVENTH WARD NATIONAL BANK,
184 Broadway, cor. of John Street.

George Montague, President.   John D. W. Grady, Cashier.

52

GRAND CENTRAL DEPOT.

HEMPHILL, HAMLIN & CO.,
CARPETING, OIL CLOTHS, DRUGGETS, MATS, ETC.,
342 AND 344 BROADWAY, NEW YORK.

56

THE METROPOLITAN HOTEL,
BROADWAY, CROSBY AND PRINCE STREETS, NEW YORK.

AIKIN, LAMBERT & CO.,
GOLD PENS, JEWELRY, WATCHES, ETC.,
23 MAIDEN LANE, NEW YORK.

AND

ALEXANDER BROWN & SONS,

Cor. Baltimore and Calvert Sts., Baltimore.

BUY AND SELL BILLS OF EXCHANGE

ON GREAT BRITAIN & IRELAND, FRANCE, GERMANY, BELGIUM, HOLLAND,
SWITZERLAND, NORWAY, DENMARK, SWEDEN AND AUSTRALIA.

ISSUE COMMERCIAL & TRAVELERS' CREDITS
IN STERLING,

Available in any part of the world, and in FRANCS, for use in Martinique and
Guadaloupe.

MAKE TELEGRAPHIC TRANSFERS OF MONEY BETWEEN THIS
COUNTRY AND EUROPE.—

*Make Collections of Drafts drawn abroad on all points in the United
States and Canada, and of Drafts drawn in the United States
on Foreign Countries.*

TO TRAVELERS.—Travelers' Credits issued either against cash deposit-
ed or satisfactory guarantee of repayment; in Dollars, for use in the United
States and adjacent countries; or in Pounds Sterling, for use in any part of the
world. Application for credits may be addressed to either of the above houses
direct, or through any first-class Bank or Banker.

BROWN, SHIPLEY & CO.,   **BROWN, SHIPLEY & CO.,**
26 Chapel Street, LIVERPOOL.   *Founder's Court, LOTHBURY, LON.*

THE BANK OF THE STATE OF NEW YORK,
State Safe Deposit Vault,
Cor. Exchange Place and William Street, New York.

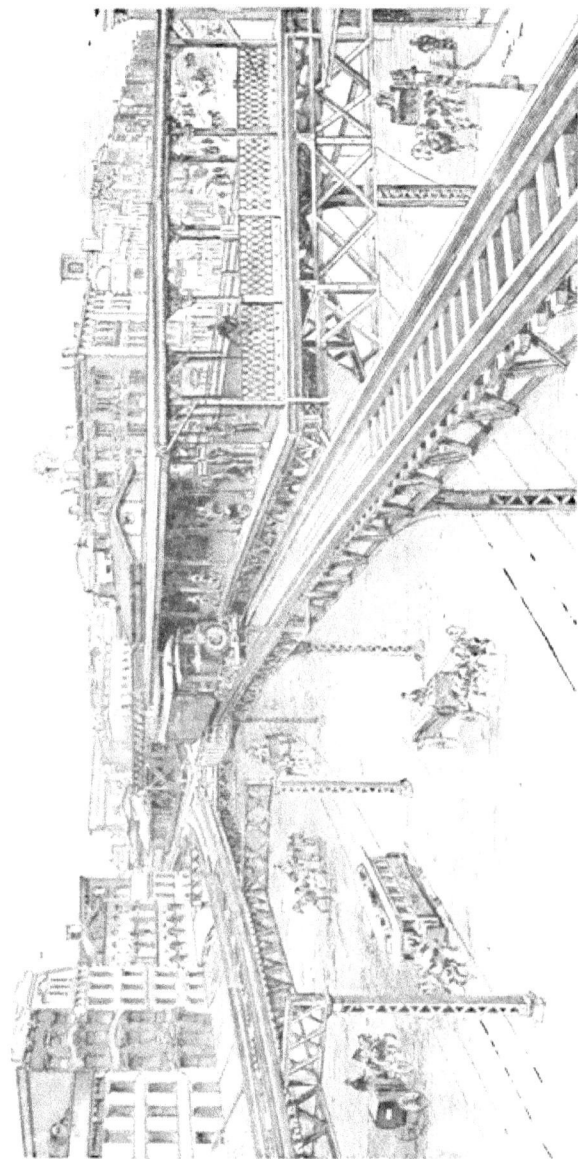

SECTION OF METROPOLITAN ELEVATED RAILROAD.

CHATHAM SQUARE.

Union Trust Company of New York,

No. 73 Broadway, Cor. Rector St.

CAPITAL, ... $1,000,000.

Has Special **Facilities for Acting as**

TRANSFER AGENT AND REGISTRAR OF DEEDS

Authorized by law to act as Executor, Administrator, Guardian, **Receiver, or Trustee, and** as a *LEGAL DEPOSITORY FOR MONEY.*

Interest allowed on Deposits, which may be made and withdrawn at any time.
N. B.—Checks on this institution pass through the Clearing House.

EDWARD KING, President.   J. M. McLEAN, 1st Vice-Pres't.
JAMES H. OGILVIE, 2d Vice-Pres't.   A. O. RONALDSON, Secretary.

The Metropolitan Plate Glass Ins. Co. of N. Y.

$100,000 in Government Bonds deposited with the Insurance Department **of the State of New** York for the protection of Policy Holders.

Cash Capital in Government Bonds $100,000.   Surplus $75,000.

Insures Plate Glass against Loss or Damage by Accidents in Stores, Dwellings, **Transit, etc.**

Principal Office, 61 LIBERTY ST., near Broadway, N. Y. City.

Henry Harteau, President.   Edgar W. Crowell, Vice-President.
Thos. S. Thore, Treasurer.   John H. Taylor, Secretary.

Vanderpoel, Green & Cuming,

Attorneys and Counsellors at Law,

United Bank Building, cor. Broadway and Wall St.,

NEW YORK.

Sidney Ward,

ATTORNEY AND COUNSELLOR,

120 Broadway, New York.

Wells, Fargo & Co.,

No. 65 BROADWAY.

BUY AND SELL MINING STOCKS AND OTHER PACIFIC COAST SECURITIES; SELL EXCHANGE, TELEGRAPHIC TRANSFERS AND CREDITS AVAILABLE THROUGHOUT THE WEST AND EUROPE, AND FORWARD FREIGHT PACKAGES AND VALUABLES TO ALL PARTS OF THE WORLD.

PATERSON, DOWNING & CO.,
Dealers in Naval Stores,
154 Front Street.

CONTINENTAL
FIRE INSURANCE CO.

George T. Hope, President.

Cyrus Peck, Secretary.

Hatch & Foote,

BANKERS AND BROKERS,

12 WALL STREET, NEW YORK.

Queen Fire Insurance Co.
OF LONDON,
37 AND 39 WALL STREET.

JAS. A. MACDONALD, - - - - - - Manager.

AMERICAN INSURANCE CO.,
OF BOSTON.

ORGANIZED 1818.

R. O. Glover, Agent, 61 WILLIAM ST., NEW YORK.

MILLS & GIBB
IMPORTERS OF LACES, EMBROIDERIES, WHITE GOODS, LINENS, ETC.,
BROADWAY AND GRAND STREET.

GARDEN CITY HOTEL,
GARDEN CITY, LONG ISLAND.

POPULAR SUMMER RESORTS

along its line than any other railroad running out of New York.

LAKE, STREAM AND MOUNTAIN SCENERY.————————

————————— - *NO MALARIA, NO MOSQUITOS.*

Write or apply for particulars.

J. BUCKLEY,
General Eastern Passenger Agent,
401 BROADWAY, N. Y.

JNO. N. ABBOTT,
General Passenger Agent,
N. Y.

FRED'K VIETOR & ACHELIS,
IMPORTERS OF WOOLENS, SILKS, HOSIERY, ETC.,
66 TO 72 LEONARD STREET.

Wall Street National Bank,

(MILLS BUILDING.) ,

Capital,	- - -		$500,000
Undivided Profits, -	· -	-	112,500

THOMAS W. EVANS, *President.*

CORNELIUS F. TIMPSON, *Vice-President.*

JOHN P. DICKINSON, *Cashier.*

J. & W. SELIGMAN & CO.

BANKERS

MILLS BUILDING,

15 BROAD STREET, NEW YORK.

ISSUE LETTERS OF CREDIT FOR TRAVELERS,

Payable in any part of Europe, Asia, Africa, Australia and America.

DRAW BILLS OF EXCHANGE

—AND MAKE—

TELEGRAPHIC TRANSFERS OF MONEY ON EUROPE AND CALIFORNIA.

MILLS BUILDING,
BROAD STREET AND EXCHANGE PLACE.

IMPORTANT ANNOUNCEMENT.

⟶⊹THE⊹⟵

UNITED STATES

LIFE INSURANCE CO.

IN THE CITY OF NEW YORK,

(ORGANIZED IN 1850,)

261, 262 & 263 Broadway, New York.

T. H. BROSNAN, President.

C. P. FRALEIGH,	A. WHEELWRIGHT,	GEO. H. BURFORD,
Secretary.	*Ass't Secretary.*	*Actuary.*

By a recent Act of the Legislature of this State this Company's charter was so amended that hereafter all the profits shall belong to the policy-holders exclusively.

All Policies henceforth issued are incontestable for any cause after three years.

Death Claims paid at once as soon as satisfactory proofs are received at the Home Office.

Absolute security, combined with the largest liberality, assures the popularity and success of this Company.

All forms of Tontine Policies issued.

☞ **GOOD AGENTS**, desiring to represent the Company, are invited to address J. S. GAFFNEY, Superintendent of Agencies, at Home Office.

THE WINDSOR HOTEL,
SARATOGA SPRINGS, N. Y.

STOCK EXCHANGE,
BROAD STREET.

NEW YORK CITY.

To the unreflecting mind it looks almost incredible that this great Empire City, with over a million of population, was founded a little more than two centuries ago.

In 1609 Hendric Hudson discovered Manhattan Island. The Island was then inhabited by a race of savages, and was an unreclaimed wilderness. In 1614 a company of Dutch traders obtained a charter from the States-General of Holland to trade with the people inhabiting the New Netherlands. It was some time after that a colony erected a few scattered dwellings near the present site of Battery Park, and christened the settlement New Amsterdam. This name it retained until the Dutch surrendered to the English in 1664, when the name was changed to New York, in honor of the Duke of York.

The whole Island was purchased from the Indians in 1624, for the sum of sixty guilders, which represents about twenty-four dollars. Not until after the Revolution did the city begin to increase perceptibly in population. Then the establishment of peace, and the dawn of the nation's liberty, gave an impetus to trade with foreign countries, and insured a steady growth of population.

The city is sixteen miles in length, extending from the Battery on the south to Yonkers City and Westchester County lines at the north, and varies in width from a few hundred yards on the southern front to four and a half miles at its widest parts, being about forty-one and a half square miles in area, or 26,560 acres, of which about nineteen square miles was annexed from the County of Westchester a few years ago. The first charter of the city was granted in 1686, by James II., king of England, and the second by George II., in 1730, which remained until 1827, when the Legislature of the State of New York granted another charter, which though variously amended, is still, in a limited degree, the basis of the existing law.

Its commercial supremacy makes it the depository and sales-room of the vast factories of New England and the Middle States. Its situation upon the Hudson, the great highway of the Empire State, early made the city the rendezvous of merchants and traders from far and near, the opening of the Erie Canal and the New York Central Railroad at grades but a little above tide-level, have been the means of pouring the products of our vast grain and grazing fields of the West in constantly increasing streams into our own and the markets of the world. With these advantages, and with nearly all other ports on the Atlantic seaboard practically cut off from our great factories of the East and the grain-growing and grazing fields of the West by the natural barriers of our mountain systems, almost or quite beyond competition, what wonder then, with such a harbor open to the ocean, that our metropolis is the commercial centre of the world.

POSTAL TELEGRAPH COMPANY,
49 Broadway.

THE NEW ST. PATRICK'S CATHEDRAL,
FIFTH AVENUE.

CENTRAL PARK.

Central Park is always a point of central attraction for visitors coming to New York. It is one of the most popular resorts of its kind in the world. It possesses attractions of such a varied character as to make its reputation a national one.

The length of the Park is about two and a half miles, from 59th street to 110th street, and about half a mile wide between Fifth and Eighth avenues, and contains 862 acres. The length of carriage-drives is about ten miles, the bridle-paths eight miles, and length of walks about thirty miles.

To see Central Park, to appreciate its kaleidoscopic beauties, would consume much unnecessary time and labor, if the visitor were not already familiar with the points of interest to see and how to see them. That this want may be supplied, the following places are noted as of especial interest :

The Gallery of Statuary and Art, Flower Gardens, Museum of Natural History on Eighth avenue, the Terrace, the Belvidere Tower, the Mall, where music may be enjoyed every Saturday afternoon if the weather is fine ; here, also, may be seen the bronze statues of the Indian Hunter and Dog, the poets Halleck, Burns, Scott and Shakespeare ; adjacent to the Mall are the Playgrounds and Carousel, marble arch, and the adjacent stone ballustered stairways, wonderfully wrought in animals, birds, vines and foliage ; near the foot of the stairway is the lake and boat-landing ; in the centre of the intervening court is the great bronze fountain.

Then, also, there are the statues of Humboldt, Morse, Moore, Mazzini and Webster. The Obelisk, as a matter of course, must be seen and admired. It stands near the 79th street and Fifth avenue entrance to the Park, and notwithstanding its great age and long journey, is as erect and symmetrical as a growing reed on the banks of the Nile. In fact it is a model of monumental architecture and proportion. The Metropolitan Museum of Art and the Sybil's Cave are but a short distance from the Obelisk. There are many attractions in the Park which we have not space to enumerate ; the visitor will meet them at every turn, and should any desire, any of the numerous park-keepers will give the directions required.

RESERVOIR,

FIFTH AVENUE, 40TH AND 42D STREETS.

STREET CAR LINES.

Broadway and Broome Street.—From **Broadway** and **Broome** street, to **Greene** street, and thence by same route as Broadway and Barclay street line. Returns by same route. **Last car leaves Central Park 11** P.M.; last car leaves Broome street **11.30** P.M.

Broadway and University Place.—From Broadway and **Barclay** street to Church street, to **Canal** street, to Greene street, to Clinton place, to **University place**, to Union **square**, to Broadway, to Seventh avenue, to 59th street, to **Central Park**. Returns by the same route to University place, to Wooster street, crosses Canal street to West **Broadway**, to College Place, to Barclay street, to starting point. Last car leaves **Central Park 11** P.M.; last car leaves Barclay street **11.45** P.M.

Eighth Avenue.—From **Broadway** and **Vesey** street, to Church street, to Chambers street, to West **Broadway**, to Canal street, to Hudson street, to Eighth avenue, to Macomb's Dam. Returns by the same route to Chambers street, to Vesey street, to Broadway. This line runs every fifteen minutes all night.

Eighth Avenue, Broadway and Canal Street.—From **Broadway** and **Canal** street, to Hudson street, thence up and down same route as Eighth avenue line, returning to Canal street and Broadway. Last car leaves Broadway and Canal street at **11** P.M.; last car leaves 49th street depot at **10.30** P.M.

Fourth Avenue.—From **Broadway** opposite Astor House, through Park Row to Centre street, to Grand street, to Bowery, to **Fourth avenue**, to Grand Central Depot, up Madison avenue to 86th street. Every third **car** continues through 32d street, to Lexington avenue, to 34th street, to Hunter's Point **Ferry**. Returns by same route to **Broome** street, to Centre street, to starting point. **Last** car leaves **Astor House 12** P.M.; last car leaves 34th street depot **11** P.M.

Ninth Avenue.—From **Broadway** and Fulton street, to Greenwich street, to **Ninth avenue, to 54th street**. Returns by the same route to Washington street, to Fulton **street**, to **Broadway**. Last car leaves Broadway corner of Fulton street **10** P.M.; **last** car leaves 54th street depot **9** P.M.

Second Avenue.—From foot of Peck Slip, **South** street, through Oliver street to Bowery, to Grand street, to Christie street, to East Houston street, to **Second avenue**, to 128th street, Harlem. Returns by Second avenue to 23d street, to First avenue, to East Houston street, to Bowery, to Chatham street, to Pearl street, to starting **point**. Also from Broadway at Astor place, to Stuyvesant street, to Second avenue, to 92d street, to East River. Returns by same route. Cars run from Peck Slip all night. Cars run from 63d street all night. Last car leaves Harlem **1** A.M.; last car leaves 63d street for Harlem **12.30** A.M. This line runs also to Broadway *via* Worth street.

WELLES BUILDING,
18 Broadway.

STREET CAR LINES—Continued.

Seventh Avenue.—From Broadway and Park Place to Church street, to Canal street, to Sullivan street, to Amity street, to Macdougal street, to Clinton place, to Greenwich avenue, to Seventh avenue, to 59th street and Central Park. Returns by same route to Sullivan street, to West Broadway, to College place, to Barclay street, to Broadway. Last car leaves Central Park at 10.30 P.M.; last car leaves Broadway at 11.15 P. M.

Sixth Avenue.—From Broadway and Vesey street, to Church street, to Chambers street, to West Broadway, to Canal street, to Varick street, to Carmine street, to Sixth avenue, to 59th street and Central Park. Returns by the same route to West Broadway, to College Place, to Vesey street, to corner of Broadway. Runs all night.

Sixth Avenue, Broadway and Canal Street.—From Broadway and Canal street, to Varick street, thence by same route as Sixth avenue line. Returns by same route. Last car leaves 43d street depot at 10.15 P.M.; last car leaves Broadway and Canal street at 10.50 P.M.

Third Avenue.—From Broadway opposite Astor House, through Park Row to Chatham street, to Bowery, to Third avenue, to 65th street, thence to Harlem. Returns by same route. Also from Broadway opposite Astor House, to Grand Central Depot. Also to Broadway and Worth street. Cars on this line run all night.

STAGE LINES.

Broadway, Twenty-third Street and Ninth Avenue Line.—Leaves South Ferry, through Broadway to 23d street, through 23d street to Ninth avenue, up Ninth avenue to 30th street. Returns same route. Fare five cents.

Broadway and Fifth Avenue Line.—Leaves Fulton Ferry, through Fulton street, to Broadway, to 14th street, to Fifth avenue, to 47th street. Returns same route. Fare five cents.

Madison Avenue Line.—Leaves Wall Street Ferry, through Wall street to Broadway, to 23d street, to Madison avenue, to 42d street, Grand Central Depot. Returns same route. Fare five cents. These stages do not run Sundays or after midnight.

FERRIES.

Astoria, foot East 92d street.
Brooklyn, Catherine Slip to Main street.
Brooklyn, foot of Fulton to Fulton street.
Brooklyn, foot of Wall street to Montague street.
Brooklyn, foot of Whitehall street to Atlantic street and Hamilton avenue.
Brooklyn (E. D.), foot of Roosevelt street to Broadway.
Brooklyn (E. D.), foot of East Houston to Grand street.
Brooklyn (E. D.), foot of Grand street to Broadway.

THE COLONNADE HOTEL,
Nos. 31, 33, 35, 37 & 39 Lafayette Place.

FERRIES—Continued.

Communipaw, foot of Liberty street.
Greenpoint, foot of East 10th street.
Hamilton avenue, foot of Whitehall street to Atlantic Dock.
Harlem, foot of Pier 24, East River.
Hoboken, foot of Barclay street.
Hoboken, foot of Christopher street.
Hunter's Point, foot of East 34th street.
Hunter's Point, foot of James' Slip to Ferry street and foot of 7th street.
Jersey City, foot of Courtlandt street to Exchange place.
Jersey City, foot of Desbrosses street to Exchange place.
Jersey City, foot of West 23d street to Pavonia ave.
Jersey City, foot of Chambers street, North River, to Pavonia avenue.
Mott Haven, Pier 22, East River.
Staten Island (Tompkinsville, Stapleton and Vanderbilt Landing), foot of Whitehall street.
Staten Island (New Brighton, S. S. Harbor, Castleton, Port Richmond), from Battery
Weehawken, foot of West 42d street.

DISTANCES IN THE CITY OF NEW YORK.

From Battery.	From Custom H.	From City Hall.		
¼ Miles.......			To	Rector st.
½ "	¼ Miles........		"	Fulton st.
¾ "	½ "		"	City Hall.
1 "	¾ "	½ Miles........	"	L'nard st.
1¼ "	1 "	¾ "	"	Canal st.
1½ "	1¼ "	1 "	"	Spring st.
1¾ "	1½ "	1¼ "	"	E. Hous'n
2 "	1¾ "	1½ "	"	E. 4th st.
2¼ "	2 "	1¾ "	"	E. 9th st.
2½ "	2¼ "	2 "	"	E. 14th st.
2¾ "	2½ "	2¼ "	"	E. 19th st.
3 "	2¾ "	2½ "	"	E. 24th st.
3¼ "	3 "	2¾ "	"	E. 29th st.
3½ "	3¼ "	3 "	"	E. 34th st.
3¾ "	3½ "	3¼ "	"	E. 38th st.
4 "	3¾ "	3½ "	"	E. 44th st.
4¼ "	4 "	3¾ "	"	E. 49th st.
4½ "	4¼ "	4 "	"	E. 54th st.
4¾ "	4½ "	4¼ "	"	E. 58th st.
5 "	4¾ "	4½ "	"	E. 63d st.
5¼ "	5 "	4¾ "	"	E. 68th st.
5½ "	5¼ "	5 "	"	E. 73d st.
5¾ "	5½ "	5¼ "	"	E. 78th st.
6 "	5¾ "	5½ "	"	E. 83d st.
6¼ "	6 "	5¾ "	"	E. 88th st.
6½ "	6¼ "	6 "	"	E. 93d st.
6¾ "	6½ "	6¼ "	"	E. 97th st.
7 "	6¾ "	6½ "	"	E. 102d st.
7¼ "	7 "	6¾ "	"	E. 107th st.
7½ "	7¼ "	7 "	"	E. 112th st.
7¾ "	7½ "	7¼ "	"	E. 117th st.
8 "	7¾ "	7½ "	"	E. 121st st.
8¼ "	8 "	7¾ "	"	E. 126th st.

HARRIGAN & HART'S
THEATRE COMIQUE.

THE COLONNADE HOTEL,
726 BROADWAY.

R. H. PARKS & CO.,

BANKERS AND BROKERS,

STOCKS, GRAIN, COTTON, Etc

13 New Street & 72 Broadway,

NEW YORK.

We have an Exclusively Private Wire to Chicago.

THE W. J. WILCOX COMPANY,

LARD REFINERY,

NEW YORK.

SALE OFFICE,

No. 41 Broad Street.

PRODUCE EXCHANGE.
Broadway and Whitehall, Beaver and Stone Streets.

INDEX.

Auctioneers, ... 4	Insurance, Fire, . . 56, 66, 68, 80
Bag and Sack Manufacturers, . . 4	Insurance, Life, . . 68, 74
Banks, Foreign, ... 12	Insurance, Marine, . . . 44, 56
Banks, National, 6, 8, 10, 50, 72	Insurance, Plate Glass, . . . 64
Banks, Savings, . . . Cover 3	Iron Merchants, ... 42
Banks, State, . . . 10, 12, 96	Iron Works, ... 62
Bankers, . . 14, 18, 20, 60, 72, 76	Jewelers, Manufacturing, . . 50, 58
Bankers and Brokers, . 22, 26, 66, 90	Kerosene Lamps and Burners, . 30
Bedding, ... 30	Kid Glove Importers, . . . 48
Blue Stone, ... 52	Land and Cattle Co., . . . 42
Bolting Cloth, . . . 32	Lard Refiners, ... 90
Bottle Caps, ... 96	Lawyers, ... 64
Brass and Copper Tubes, . 30, 52	Lead Pencil Manufacturers, . 62
Brass and Copper Wires, 30, 52	Lumber, Ship, Car and Wagon, . 58, 80
Brokers, Grain and Provision, . 90	Oils, Illuminating, . . . 68
Brokers, Petroleum, . . . 38	Photographic Materials, . 62
Brokers, Stock, ... 76	Pianoforte Manufacturers, . 62
Burglar Alarm, Automatic, . . 40	Powder Manufacturers, . . 36
Carriage Material, . . 38, 80	Railway Companies, . . . 70
Cements, Enameled Bricks, . 40	Refiners of Petroleum, . . 52
Champagne, Wines, Importers, . 54	Rock Drills, ... 36
Chemicals, Importers and Dealers, . 34	Salt and Fish, ... 34
Chemists, Manufacturing, . . 34	Safes, ... 16
China, Importers French, . 32	Safe Deposit Co., . 16, 80, Cover 2
China and Japan Goods, . 32	Scales, ... 54
Coffees and Teas, . . . 32	Schiedam Schnapps, . . 38
Collar and Cuff Manufacturers, . 38	Shipping and Commission Merchants, 58
Combs and Bracelets, . . 38	Soda and Saleratus, . . 34
Diamond Importers, . . 50, 58	Soda Water Apparatus Manufacturers, 34
Dress Goods Importers, . . 48	Steam Pumps, ... 68
Dry Goods Jobbers, . . 48	Steamship Companies, . . 58
Elevators, ... 30	Steel Castings, Steel Tools, . 36
Express Forwarders, . 64	Storage Warehouses, . . 34
Fancy Goods Importers, 62	Tin Foil Manufacturers, . 96
Fire Alarm and Extinguisher, 40	Toys, China and Fancy Goods, . 48
Fire-Brick Works, . . 54	Trust Companies, . . . 44, 64
Fire-Works Manufacturers, . 54	Umbrella and Parasol Manufacturers, 24
Fish, Salt and Salt Fish, . 54	Varnish and Japan Manufacturers, . 42
Fur Dealers and Furriers, . 48	Wines, Brandies and Liquors, . 36
Gas Fixtures, . . 62	Wire Cloth, ... 42
Hollow Bricks, . . 42	Woods, Foreign and Domestic, . 68
Insurance, Fidelity, . 24	Wood-Working Machinery, . 52

92

VIEW DOWN BROADWAY.

LIST OF PROMINENT BUILDINGS.

	PAGE.
THE STEWART WAREHOUSE BUILDING,	5
LIVERPOOL & LONDON & GLOBE INSURANCE CO.,	7
UNITED BANK BUILDING,	9
MARINE NATIONAL BANK,	13
CENTURY BUILDING,	15
POST OFFICE,	17
THE GRAND UNION HOTEL, SARATOGA SPRINGS, N. Y.,	19
STANDARD OIL CO.'S BUILDING,	21
HALSTED, HAINES & CO.,	23
THE BARBOUR BROTHERS CO.'S MILLS.	28
THE STEWART OFFICE BUILDING,	29, 31
THE PARK AVENUE HOTEL,	35
MITCHELL, VANCE & CO.,	37
BATES, REED & COOLEY,	39
GALLATIN NATIONAL BANK,	43
INSURANCE BUILDINGS,	45
GEORGE H. CLARK & CO.,	46
TEFFT, WELLER & CO.,	49
SEVENTH WARD BANK,	51
GRAND CENTRAL DEPOT,	53
HEMPHILL, HAMLIN & CO.,	55
THE METROPOLITAN HOTEL,	57
AIKIN, LAMBERT & CO.,	59
THE BANK OF THE STATE OF NEW YORK,	61
PATERSON, DOWNING & CO.,	65
MILLS & GIBB,	67
GARDEN CITY HOTEL,	69
FRED'K VIETOR & ACHELIS,	71
MILLS BUILDING,	73
WINDSOR HOTEL, SARATOGA SPRINGS, N. Y.,	75
STOCK EXCHANGE,	77
POSTAL TELEGRAPH,	79
CATHEDRAL,	81
RESERVOIR,	83
WELLES BUILDING,	85
COLONNADE HOTEL,	87
COLONNADE HOTEL AND THEATRE COMIQUE,	89
PRODUCE EXCHANGE,	91
VAN VLECK & CO.'S SAILING VESSEL, "GOV. ROBIE,"	27

94

TERRACE AND FOUNTAIN.
CENTRAL PARK.

www.ingramcontent.com/pod-product-compliance
Lightning Source LLC
Chambersburg PA
CBHW032248080426
42735CB00008B/1058